Peer Pressure

Nyachin C. Thian

Copyright © 2022 Nyachin C. Thian

Published by CaryPress International Books
www.CaryPress.com

All rights reserved.

No part of this publication may be reproduced, distributed, or transmitted in any form or by any means, including photocopying, recording, or other electronic or mechanical methods, without the prior written permission of the publisher, except in the case of brief quotations embodied in critical reviews and certain other noncommercial uses permitted by copyright law.

Chapter 1

Our craft class adventures started a few months ago when I was on the train with Dad. He always had crossword puzzles and other things to stay busy to pass the time on the train and I enjoyed helping him solve these puzzles.

"I'm pretty sure you need Q-U-E for that, dad!" I said as he tried spelling Mozambique. I've always been very good at long-spelling words.

"You sure *sure*?" Dad asked with a smile. Our conversation was interrupted when we heard someone get up puzzled and say, "have I missed my stop?! Oh no! I have…"

"Where do you need to get off?" Dad asked.

"Broadway," the lady apprehensively added.

"Oh, that's the next stop. You're good."

The lady sighed and said, "Thank God. I was worried about missing an event I'm headed to. The Pop-Up Read n Craft Center I volunteer with moved spots."

"That's where we are going too," I interjected, then I looked at Dad anxiously to see if I would be in trouble for talking to a stranger, but he didn't look concerned.

Instead, he offered to help, "You can walk with us if you like."

"Thank you. I'll do that, as I have heard it's easy to get lost there."

Dad nodded in agreement.

***

Getting off the train, the lady introduced herself, "I'm Heather, by the way. Thank you for helping me find my way here." It was a busy street, so we all picked up our pace.

"I'm Douglas. Nice to meet you. This is my daughter, Ayala."

"Same here. So, do you come to the Pop-Up Read n Craft Center often?" She directed her attention to me, making me a little nervous.

"Uhh, sometimes we come here. Dad says I need to build my library collection and share it with the neighborhood kids." I added timidly.

When we arrived at the Center, children of all ages and their parents had animated conversations with the volunteers giving away coloring books and markers.

I browsed through the collections of coloring books. It was always easy to find something interesting to color. I chose one, said our goodbyes to Ms. Heather, and walked with Dad towards a Farmer's Market a few blocks away.

Chapter 2

I don't know if we would have found out about the craft classes if it hadn't been for Ms. Heather. After we left the Farmer's Market, we ran into her again at the station.

"Douglas! Ayala!" Ms. Heather exclaimed, waving her hand wildly. She had a big grin on her face. "I'm so happy I ran into you again."

"Do you need some more help with the train?" my Dad asked, chuckling.

"Hah! I like you, Douglas. You're funny," she said. "Actually, I wanted to invite you to this craft class I'm hosting. It's through my program Tribe Vibe. They're open to anyone, adults, *and* kids, and totally free."

My Dad looked interested, nodding his head, but I felt my insides squirm. He looked at me. "What do you think, Sunshine? Do you want to try?"

I crossed my arms. I didn't want to disappoint my Dad, but I wasn't sure I liked the idea. I tried to think of an excuse. "I'm not very good at craft…."

"You don't have to be super artsy," Ms. Heather reassured me. "It's for anyone in the community to join and have fun. Think about it, but I am certain you'll enjoy it if you come. Let me give you my phone number in case you decide to try it."

Ms. Heather gave us the event details and walked away with a wave.

***

On the day of the first craft class, I was so nervous! Butterflies and all kinds of other flying creatures fluttered in my stomach. I knew Ms. Heather said it was for anyone, but I didn't know what to expect. It was scary.

I only agreed to go because my Dad seemed excited to try it together. That was the kind of Dad he was. He always loved doing things with me, and he always encouraged me to get out of my comfort zone and try new things. I glanced at my Dad as we walked to the building. He gave me an encouraging smile.

"I think this will be fun," he said.

I couldn't help but mirror back his smile. I took a deep breath. Yes, it was scary, but I knew Dad would always be there for me.

As soon as we walked in, we were met with Ms. Heather's warm smile. "I'm so glad you both made it! Can I give you hugs?"

I was a little surprised, but I figured it couldn't hurt after my Dad hugged her. So, I hugged her too. I was surprised as I let go. It helped. I felt my shoulders relax.

Dad let me pick seats in the back, which helped too. It felt easier to breathe. Dad talked to me, but I had a hard time listening as I took everything and everyone in. There weren't many people there but enough that it made the small room feel full. And there were still others walking in. All kinds of people sat around me—old like my grandma and a couple of kids who looked younger than me, both boys and girls. And everyone was smiling.

The classes were for anyone, after all. That, too, made me feel better.

***

It didn't take long for me to get overwhelmed, though. After Ms. Heather made introductions and gave us instructions, it was time to start puppet making. Although no one said anything to me, I felt pressured to pick out fabric quickly. I picked out one with green polka dots. When I sat down and started cutting it, I began second-guessing my choice.

"You picked a good fabric," Dad complimented me. He was slowly cutting his solid blue fabric.

I wrinkled my nose. I knew what he was trying to do—he was just saying that to make me feel better.

Focusing on my project, I fell into a rhythm. My worries and the whole world fell away for a moment. All that mattered was the puppet. I tied on the hands and added a top crossbar.

"Wow! Look at that girl's puppet, Mommy!" a little girl behind me said.

I peeked around to see that she was pointing at my puppet. A burst of pride filled me. I looked at my puppet, though, and grimaced. *It wasn't right.* One arm was longer than the other, and its head was tilted.

After we finished and said goodbye to Ms. Heather, Dad and I used the crossbars to make the puppets walk their way to the train stop.

"Did you have fun?" Dad asked me, swinging his puppet gently into mine. I laughed. It looked like his puppet was trying to wrestle mine.

"I guess so," I said. I swung mine back at his. Soon, we were both laughing, and the puppets' strings were tangled together.

"I think I want to go to the next craft class," he said as we tried to pull the strings apart. "Would you come with me? Maybe we can bring Jacob."

I focused on untying a tricky knot to have time to think. I remembered the worry I had initially, but then, I recalled how it disappeared at some point. I also remembered the little girl who liked my puppet, even if it wasn't perfect.

"Okay," I said finally. "We can try again."

Chapter 3

Knock, knock.

"Your twin is here!" Dad jokingly referred to Jacob as my twin. He was not only my BFF, but our next door neighbor as well. We were siblings from two mothers. Our families did a lot of stuff together. As we sat at the dinner table doing our homework, I moved the hot cocoa mug towards him.

"When did you get those?" Jacob took a sip and admired the colorful craft.

"You know the craft class I told you about. Dad and I made them last week." The second craft class was a coffee mug project. It was cool to shape it and then glaze it in a kiln. The third craft class was an angel-making project using coffee filters and pipe cleaners. Aside from the artistic expression, it had been a mixed experience. I still wasn't sure if it was the right hobby for me. Many distractions overwhelmed me and created social anxiety.

I could tell Jacob was envious. "These are so cool!"

"Would you like to join us for the next class?"

"Let me ask my mom!" He put the pencil down and zoomed out the door. He lived next door, so it was easier to ask to go there rather than call on the phone. "Mom said yeah but wants to make sure that your dad is okay with that too."

"Let me ask dad when he comes back from the store."

***

The next day at lunchtime, I dashed to find my bestie. "Jacob over here," I gestured with my hand to get him a seat near me in the cafeteria. "Guess what! My Dad said you can come over to our house Friday so we can all go to Ms. Heather's class."

"Really?! Yay!" He beamed. He was eager to go to the craft workshops offered by Crafty Kidz. In fact, he had expressed interest the moment I shared what I had done over the weekend.

Looking back, to be honest, I didn't know how I felt about the craft class the first few times that I went with Dad. My Dad had to convince me to go with him the very first time. "You'll love it, I promise," he'd said. I didn't want to hurt his feelings, but I was certain that I'd feel like a fish out of water.

When lunch ended, we put away our food trays and walked back to our class, talking about the next project that Ms. Heather had shared with the class – abstract painting using tape.

"I can't wait to tell mom that I'll be making a painting for her. She loves crafts." Jacob's enthusiasm was contagious. Now, I, too, was kind of looking forward to seeing how he made his painting.

***

Finally, it was Saturday, an craft class day for Jacob and me. I had set the alarm clock to 7 am to make sure I had time to pack my bag with lunch and a few snacks to enjoy with Jacob and Dad during our train ride.

"Good morning, Sunshine!" Dad said in his sleepy voice, "thank you for preparing extra early. I'll make French toast for you and Jacob. He should be here in a few minutes."

"Yum! I've packed some ham and cheese sandwiches, granola bars, and Gatorade for all of us," I said while braiding my hair.

"Good thinking!" and gave me a thumbs up.

Soon Jacob was having a quick breakfast with us and excitedly sharing what he wanted to paint for his mom. After washing our dishes, I grabbed my small backpack with our goodies and walked out with Dad and Jacob. He locked the door behind us, and we all walked to the Patco train station.

After walking for about twenty minutes, we got on our train and headed to Camden. The station was busier than usual, with young families and their kids heading out to enjoy their Saturday.

While Dad was getting a spot for all three of us, Jacob asked me if Ms. Heather was nice. He was a little nervous and wondered if he would like her. He explained why he was asking that question, "If a teacher is nice, then it is easy for a student to like the subject being taught."

"It's kind of like our math teacher, Ms. Smith-she's kind and helpful, so it's easy to like her class! But our social studies teacher, Mr. Flores, can be a little intimidating, so sometimes I dread that period."

"Yeah, that makes sense!" Jacob agreed.

I was grateful that he got a chance to tag along. The last few rides to the craft workshop were lonely. I was glad I had a talkative friend to keep me from getting bored in the class.

Chapter 4

By the time Ms. Heather walked to the front of the room, Jacob could not sit still in his seat. I covered my smile with my hand.

I had been the complete opposite when I had started the Crafty Kidz classes. I was worried about the unknown. I had been to a few of them before Jacob joined Dad and me, though, so I had started warming up to them. Plus, it would be even better to share it with my best friend.

"Hello, everyone!" Ms. Heather exclaimed with a big smile. "It's awesome to see returning and new faces. For those of you who don't know me, I'm Ms. Heather. I teach these classes. Just like school, but way more fun! I hope anyway."

Ms. Heather sent us a wink, and people laughed.

"Oh, good! Now, we are getting warmed up," she said, laughing along. "You passed the first test. To enjoy craft, you just need to be comfortable and be yourself. For today's class, can I have a couple of volunteers?"

Nervous, I looked away from Ms. Heather. I looked at anything but her—the ceiling, the floor, my Dad's white baseball cap. Out of the corner of my eye, I saw Jacob's hand shoot up.

"Thank you!" Ms. Heather said, looking at our table. "What's your name?"

"Jacob," my friend said confidently.

"Well, it's nice to meet you, Jacob. Do we have any other people that could volunteer?"

Something pushed into my shoulder, making me stumble off my stool and stand up.

"Ayala! Thank you so much!" Ms. Heather beamed.

I spun around to glare at Jacob. He sent me an innocent smile before pulling me to the front with him. Ms. Heather gave Jacob a stack of stock paper, gave me a roll of masking tape, and asked us to pass them out to everyone. While we did, she explained the project.

First, she presented her sample. I glanced up and admired it. It was so pretty and perfect. There were white lines in between shapes of color. Each shape had a mix of blues and greens. It reminded me of water.

"The first step will be to put tape on your paper. You can make lines across it or shapes or use none at all if you don't want. Then, you will paint across it. After it's dry, you can take the tape off, and that's how you make the white areas like on mine."

When Jacob and I were done passing the supplies out, I sat down and nervously looked at my blank sheet of paper. Jacob already had half a dozen pieces of tape stretched across his. I glanced at my Dad's. He also had a couple of pieces of tape down already.

I picked up the tape roll, broke off a piece, and laid it on the paper, top to bottom. It didn't reach all the way, though. I frowned and peeled it off carefully. I didn't want to rip the paper. I tried to put it down in a different spot, but it still wasn't right. As I peeled it off again, I felt a warm hand on my shoulder.

"How are we doing over here?" Ms. Heather asked in a bright voice.

"Great!" Jacob exclaimed, already putting a bold red stripe on his paper.

"Always a good time, Ms. Heather," my Dad said with a smile.

"You're too kind, Douglas," Ms. Heather said, patting his back. "What about you, Ayala?"

I frowned, staring at the crumpled piece of tape stuck to the palm of my hand. "I can't get it right." I covered my eyes with my right hand in frustration.

"There's no such thing as 'right' in craft," Ms. Heather replied. "Sometimes, it's messy, and that's okay. But it's okay if you need help too."

Chapter 5

As I continued the craft classes, I began to feel lighter, like maybe I could do anything. After the craft class, I tried roller skating with Dad and Jacob. The next day at school, I raised my hand in class to answer questions, something I had never done before. I don't know what changed, but I thought I liked it.

One day a while later, my class had gym at school. The gym wasn't my favorite class. I wasn't the most athletic kid, but I still thought it was fun to play sports.

After changing into our gym uniforms, the teacher, Ms. Stenstrom, led us through stretching. I followed her lead. I pulled one arm across my body, then the other. I lunged forward with one leg, then the next. I did twenty sit-ups easily! I felt like I was on a roll.

"All right, everyone, line up!" Ms. Stenstrom hollered.

I scurried to the line next to Jacob.

The gym teacher paced in front of us. "If you recall, we finished our volleyball segment yesterday. So today, we will be starting basketball."

There were whoops and shouts of excitement from many of the kids. I smiled and clapped along. Basketball was my favorite sport. Ever since I was a kid, Dad took me to the basketball court at our neighborhood park. We would play "HORSE" and one-on-one.

"I think you all know the basics of the game, but as usual, we'll go through the basics and rules of the game. First, there are two teams…."

Ms. Stenstrom continued explaining the game. When she introduced the concept of dribbling, she asked for a volunteer to show how it was done. After volunteering in craft class, I considered raising my hand. Jacob raised his and nodded at me encouragingly. I started lifting it—I knew how to dribble after all—but before I could raise it all the way, the teacher had already picked Tasha Buck, one of the starting players for the girls' basketball team.

She did the same thing with passing the ball and guarding. I raised my hand, but she chose other students, which was kind of a bummer.

"Next, let's talk about shooting!" Ms. Stenstrom continued. "Shooting is vital to the game—it's how your team scores points. But, of course, to get the points, you can't just shoot—you have to make a basket."

Ms. Stenstrom showed how to hold the ball, dominant hand underneath to push it up, and non-dominant on the side to steady it. Then, she bent her knees, jumped, and shot. The ball swished through the net.

She turned to us. "Who thinks they can do it?"

Confidently, I shot my hand up straight into the air.

"Ayala! Quick reflexes, that's great for this game," Ms. Stenstrom complimented. She motioned me forward.

Pushing my shoulders back, I moved onto the court.

Ms. Stenstrom bounce passed me the ball and instructed, "Go ahead and shoot from anywhere."

I picked a spot four or five feet away from the basket at a diagonal angle. It was my go-to spot when playing "HORSE." It wasn't too far away, and there was a nice angle to hit the backboard.

I dribbled the ball in place a couple of times, lined up the shot, bent my knees, and jumped! I pushed the ball up and watched as it sailed towards the basket—then smacked into the backboard and flew back towards me! I gasped and ducked.

"Whoa!"

I whipped my head around to see Ms. Stenstrom barely catch the ball before it hit her in the head. Frozen, I stared at her and the ball. What had just happened? How could I have missed?

Laughter burst out behind me. My cheeks started to burn.

Ms. Stenstrom called, "Nice try, Ayala! Great form, just a little less strength behind it. You'll get it next time for sure!"

I hurried back to my spot next to Jacob with my head down. Ms. Stenstrom moved on to talking about free throws, but I couldn't listen.

Jacob elbowed me and whispered, "Hey, don't worry about it. Everyone misses sometimes."

But how could I not worry about it? Everyone laughed at me. I should have never volunteered. If I hadn't, I wouldn't have been put in such an embarrassing place. And, I knew, if I never started the craft classes, I never would have volunteered.

Chapter 6

I was quiet when Dad picked me up from school.

"How was your day, Sunshine?" he asked.

I just shrugged. I didn't want to lie and say it had been a good day, but I wasn't in the mood to talk about what happened either. It was so embarrassing—I could feel my cheeks heating up just by the thought of it.

Dad knew something was wrong. He always did. Still, he didn't try to nag me about it. That wasn't how he was. He knew that I would tell him about what happened when I was ready.

Instead, he talked on and on about his jobs. He tried to lighten my mood with a funny story about a cat running wild in the mall. It *was* funny, but I couldn't laugh after what happened earlier…

"Listen, Ayala. We don't have to go to dinner tonight with Ms. Heather and Joseph if you're not up for it," Dad said.

My eyes widened two sizes bigger than normal. I had forgotten all about the dinner.

Since we started the craft classes, our families have grown close. Dad, Jacob, Ms. Heather, her husband, Joseph, and me. We started getting together outside of classes and giving each other little presents. We had gotten so close that when they learned that Dad's birthday was coming up, Ms. Heather and Joseph invited all of us to dinner to celebrate.

"No, we can go. I'm fine," I lied. I wasn't in the mood to go, but I couldn't tell him that. He deserved to have a nice birthday. I tried to give him a giant reassuring smile. He gave me a doubtful look but didn't argue it any further.

***

A couple of hours later, Dad, Jacob, and I entered the Italian restaurant where Ms. Heather told us to meet them. I looked around the foyer. The walls were painted with murals of gondola boats in Venice waterways, the Colosseum, and the Leaning Tower of Pisa.

"Whoa! Do you think they really look like that?" Jacob asked, staring at the murals.

I shrugged. My mood had not become any better since I left school.

We walked in further and saw Ms. Heather motioning us over to their table. As we did, both she and Joseph stood up and gave us hugs. Ms. Heather, Joseph, Dad, and Jacob all talked together nonstop. I was sure they didn't even notice that I hadn't said a word. But that was okay, I told myself. It was Dad's day, not mine.

I ordered spaghetti and meatballs and swirled the melting ice cubes around in my water.

"How was school today?" Ms. Heather asked Jacob and me.

Jacob stiffened and shut his mouth, becoming just as silent as me.

"Uh oh," Ms. Heather grimaced. "I don't miss *those* kinds of days at school. What happened?"

Glancing at me, Jacob hesitated. He really was a great friend. No matter how much he wanted to tell the story, he would have my back and remain silent if I didn't want to talk about it. And I didn't want to talk. Not yet.

"Never mind! Forget I asked." Ms. Heather held her hands up in surrender.

By the time the food came out, they had started talking about the next craft class. My throat tightened. I spun my spaghetti over and over around my fork.

"Is something wrong with the food, Ayala?" Joseph asked.

I shook my head. I couldn't respond, but I put a bite in my mouth for good measure.

"Well, I, for one, am very excited to paint those tote bags," Dad said, wiping his mouth with a napkin. "It will look good, *and* we can use it. What about you guys?"

Jacob nodded excitedly.

However, I knew what I had to say. I couldn't keep it in anymore. I blurted out, "I don't want to go anymore."

Chapter 7

Everyone at our table fell quiet. It was strange how everyone else in the room kept moving and talking like normal. I finally looked up to see my friends and family staring at me.

"What do you mean? I thought you liked them!" Jacob exclaimed.

"I-I did," I stammered out, not wanting to make Ms. Heather feel bad, "but I just don't want to go anymore."

"Just because you were embarrassed?" Jacob asked.

I shot him a glare, and he clamped his mouth shut.

Dad leaned over to touch my shoulder. "Of course, I won't make you go, but can we talk about it first?"

"I guess so," I said and ate a meatball.

The rest of the table started eating again, but the air was static. Maybe I should have waited to tell Dad later.

Suddenly, Ms. Heather spoke up. "You know, the other day, I had this big meeting. In the middle of it, I stopped to drink some water and somehow spilled it all over myself."

I listened carefully but didn't know what to make of her story. It did make me breathe easier, though. I looked at Dad, Jacob, and Joseph. They smiled and nodded as if the story had done the same to them. Soon after, Joseph told us a story of how he was trying to skateboard and accidentally did the splits. "Oh, I have the video of it on my cell phone as my friend was with me." We all laughed, even me when the accident scene came. Everyone started telling embarrassing stories. It made me realize that embarrassing things happen to everyone every day.

I started talking slowly until it was like any other day. Ms. Heather whispered something to the waiter, and a few minutes later, he walked out with a chocolate cake that had what looked like a hundred candles lit on top. I felt a laugh bubble out from me. Ms. Heather elbowed Dad.

"Haha, very funny. I'm not *that* old," Dad chuckled.

We sang "Happy Birthday" to him, and he tried to blow out all the candles. It took him seven tries to get them all. We ate and talked and laughed and enjoyed being together to celebrate my Dad. By the time we got up to leave, I hadn't thought about the gym class that whole time.

We walked out with Ms. Heather and Joseph.

Ms. Heather said, "Okay, I know you said you don't want to do the craft classes anymore—and that's okay! You won't hurt my feelings...but I will miss you."

I looked away but mumbled, "I will miss you, too."

"So...why not try coming one last time?" Ms. Heather suggested. "You don't have to talk or even do the project. Just come by to say hi. If you decide to do the project, even better, but no one will force you."

Frowning, I said, "I don't know…."

"Just think about it," Ms. Heather said. She wrapped her arms around me.

We all said goodbye, and Dad, Jacob, and I walked to the train station. The whole time, Jacob was trying to persuade me to reconsider. But I was sure.

Finally, once we sat down on the train, Dad spoke up. "You don't have to go anymore. I just thought they were a fun thing we could do together."

"They were," I reassured him. "I had lots of fun."

"Then, why don't you want to go anymore? What changed?" he asked. He moved his head so his concerned expression was the only thing I could see.

PEER PRESSURE

I didn't want Dad to worry. So, I finally broke down and told him about gym class. I poured my heart into every word but realized how silly it all sounded as I spoke. At the same time, though, I hated how embarrassed I had been. I didn't want to feel that way again.

"Oh, Sunshine," Dad sighed when I finished. He put an arm around my shoulders, pulling me close.

"I didn't want to say anything and ruin your birthday party," I murmured. "I know I overreacted...but I don't want to be embarrassed anymore."

"Remember the stories from dinner? We all get embarrassed," Jacob said.

"I know, you're right," I confessed.

"So, does that mean..." Jacob trailed off and gave me a toothy grin.

I wrinkled my nose. "One more craft class. But I can't promise more than that."

Chapter 8

Ms. Heather's eyes lit up in the next craft class when she saw me. She squeezed my shoulder and said, "I'm glad you decided to come."

"One last time," I reminded her.

She nodded. "Of course, one last time."

Over the few days between the gym class and craft, I had calmed down. The first day after wasn't great. Kids in my class called me Ricochet. I didn't think I spoke at all during school that day. By last class, though, Juan Rodriguez had let out a high-pitched scream when he thought he saw a mouse. Ricochet was forgotten. Still, I had promised myself I wouldn't make the mistake of putting myself out there again.

Ms. Heather walked to the front of the room. She began, "Welcome back, everyone! Today, we will be painting tote bags. You, of course, can paint and decorate it any way you desire, but if you need ideas, why not paint it with something that makes you happy."

She continued to give us instructions. Then, she asked for volunteers to help pass things out. I looked away and folded my arms over my torso. I wasn't making that mistake again.

After the volunteer handed me a tote bag, I laid it flat on the table. It was so blank and white. Staring at the emptiness, it was quite a daunting task to start. I had no idea what to paint. I peeked around the room to see everyone with paintbrushes in their hands.

I couldn't do it. Suddenly, I stood up and pulled the tote bag off the table.

"You okay, Ayala?" Jacob asked.

I shrugged. "I'm just not in the mood."

"The hardest part is starting," Dad said, looking up from his bag. He had painted the outline of a house.

"It's true," Jacob agreed. "At first, I had no clue what picture I would want to carry around. But then, I thought about what Ms. Heather said—paint what makes you happy. So, I started painting animals!"

Peering down, I saw several circles that I guessed were heads. Slowly, I sat back down and looked at the tote bag. *What makes ME happy?*

I picked up a paintbrush with a shaking hand and dipped it into the black paint. Before overthinking it, I touched the brush to the tote bag, permanently marking it. It started out as a line, then it curved. Then, I closed the line. I rinsed out my brush and picked brown as my next color.

A peace came over me. I relaxed in my chair and focused solely on my painting. I would frown when I made mistakes, but then I would take a deep breath and try again.

"Wow," Dad said. "That looks great."

Jacob's words brought me back to the present. Whatever daze had taken me vanished. I looked down at my painting. There was a kid on one side with my braids and another on the other with Jacob's closely shaved hair.

"Hey, is that me?" Jacob asked excitedly.

I laughed. "Of course, it's you. I decided to paint what makes me happy. And you're my best friend."

"You always need a good friend for when life gets crazy," Dad said with a smile. I rolled my eyes good-naturedly. He always said that like a motto. Then, he continued, "And the palette?"

I looked over to Ms. Heather. She was laughing with another student. I couldn't help but smile as I answered, "I realized craft makes me happy too."

I hugged Dad and Jacob and said, "Thanks for getting me to come back."

Chapter 9

The next Monday, I woke up to Dad's voice.

"Ayala! You're still in bed? We have to go soon!"

I peered at my bedside clock and gasped, "Oh, no!"

We needed to leave in fifteen minutes. I threw on clothes and brushed my teeth. I hurried out of the bathroom to see Dad tying up his work boots. Without looking up, he asked, "You ready?"

"Yeah, I'll just grab a granola bar to eat on the way," I huffed. Then, I grabbed one from the kitchen cabinet and found my backpack on the table. Picking it up, I swung it over my shoulder when...*smack!* I jumped at the unexpected sound right behind me. I quickly realized how light my backpack suddenly was. "No, no, no, not today..."

Spinning around, I saw all my books on the ground. I reached for the bottom of my backpack, and...yep, there was a massive hole at the bottom. I hadn't even realized it had gotten that old!

"Are you okay?" Dad asked, rushing into the kitchen. He glanced from me to the books on the ground to my backpack.

"What do I do?" I exclaimed.

Dad pursed his lips and looked around. "There's no time to get a new one before school—you'll just have to make do with something else. We have grocery bags somewhere or…actually…."

He slipped out of the room but reappeared a moment later. He smiled and held up my tote bag from craft class. My paintings of Jacob and I smiled at me too. Dad said, "I told you it could be useful."

I wasn't so sure I wanted to take it to school. My craft skills weren't great. Showing other people in craft class was one thing. We all were painting them together. However, as I learned in gym class, some kids liked to make fun of other people over anything. But we didn't have time to look for something better.

"Fine, okay," I said. I threw my books into the tote bag, and we left.

***

Walking into the school, I kept the painting side of the tote bag hidden against me. I maneuvered through the crowd of students hurrying to their first-period classes. I only had a few minutes to get to mine, and I didn't want to be late.

I jogged past my locker without stopping and headed toward math class. I had homework for it over the weekend, so I didn't need to stop and get the book. I made it into the classroom and sighed in relief. A second later, the bell rang, announcing the start of school.

I weaved my way to my desk and sat down, trying to catch my breath. I let the tote bag slide to the floor, taking my math book out.

The girl sitting next to me leaned over as the teacher took attendance. "Hey."

Glancing over, I warily said, "Hi?"

She was new to the school, only arriving a couple of weeks before. Valerie, but she went by Val. I had admired her dark curly hair and how easy she seemed to talk to everyone.

Smiling, Val pointed to the floor next to my desk. To my horror, I saw what she was looking at. My painting. I had been careless when setting it down and putting the painting side out.

I stammered, "Oh, that…."

"It's awesome! I love it. Where did you get it?"

I was shocked and silent. Looking her over, I realized she was being genuine. She liked my painting. I admitted, "Actually, I made it."

"Really?" she exclaimed. "You're so good!"

"Thanks," I laughed, trying to hide my embarrassment at the sudden praise. "I actually made it at a craft class. Maybe you could check it out and make one yourself."

"That would be so cool!"

I gave her the details of the next Crafty Kidz class, and she asked if she could sit with me at lunch. I couldn't believe it. It looked like my craft may have helped me make a new friend.

Chapter 10

"All right, everyone, let's begin our apple painting class. And let me show you what mine turned out to be," Ms. Heather took out a beautifully painted, golden baby apple with a glittery stem.

It was gorgeous, and I was mesmerized by it. "I want mine to be the same!" I whispered to Dad and Jacob.

"Well, I want mine different," Jacob said emphatically, reaching for blue and purple colors and spreading them on his apple lavishly.

Dad chuckled and nodded. "Let's see what mine turns out to be."

After half an hour of tinkering with different colors, I was starting to feel less hopeful that my project would be as beautiful as the craft teacher's. I tried getting Dad's attention to get his opinion. He looked at it and blurted, "not bad!". I think he was trying to be nice and not hurt my feelings.

"Ms. Heather, may I be excused? I need to go to get some water."

"Sure, sweetheart."

I thought of hiding my apple in my pocket and throwing it away in the trash can. But that would leave paint marks on my clothes. I just needed a few minutes from the class to think about my next steps. I left the room and stopped at the water fountain to get a sip of water. I wanted to spend a little more time alone as I wasn't ready to submit my project yet. I walked up and down the stairs two times. Took another sip of water and then took a long sigh and decided to return to the classroom. Dad looked concerned that I took longer than usual.

His apple was yellow and green. Jacob's was blue and purple. I decided to give it another try before calling it finished. After mixing red, yellow, and orange, I re-paint it to make it look like a sunrise.

"Oh, that looks good!" Jacob said.

"Really?"

"Yeah. It reminds me of the sunrise."

"Yeah, it does look like that. Let me see yours…Ohh, those silver stars look awesome! Hey! I'll call my craft Sunrise, and yours can be called the Starry Night!"

"We are total opposites," he giggled, and I couldn't help giggling out loud in the class with him. That's the first time I've ever done that! Made that fearless laughter sound. It felt so good. Dad looked at me with a smile and winked.

Soon everyone was able to show off their finished work, and Ms. Heather oohed and ahhed everyones' apples. Then it was my turn, and her eyes shone as if my apple was a rising sun like the name I had chosen.

"Call me biased, but I think yours is the star of this show, hands down," she said and started clapping. The whole class joined her, and something happened in that magical moment for me. I felt something rising out of me like the sun.

I felt as if I had grown 12 inches taller.

***

Ms. Heather asked us to stay after the class was over. Once the last person left class, she gave Dad and me a gift bag. His had orange stripes on it, and mine was blue and sparkly. "It's nothing big, but I wanted to give you a gift."

She encouraged us to open them, so we did. She gave me a brand-new sketch notebook. I smiled and thought it was such a nice gift. Then, I looked at Dad. He was holding a rock that was as big as his hand. On the top was written the word "Joyful" in gold paint.

"Let me explain," Ms. Heather said. "The sketchbook is to remind you that anyone can be an artist. And well, the rock says what it represents. I kept it on my desk for over a year, and it encouraged and inspired me to be joyful: to try new things, stretch my limits, and inspire others. I hope the rock can bring joy to you too."

My Dad said thank you, and we hugged Ms. Heather goodbye. Dad put the Joyful rock on our porch table with houseplants next to our front door when we got home.

"Why are you putting it out here?" I asked him.

He responded, "I think it's important to share the rock with other people too. So, they can also experience joy."

"But what if it gets ruined by the rain?" I wondered.

He shrugged and smiled. "Then, we can paint 'Joyful' on again."

After a while, the word started to fade, so we did just that. We painted the word again in white with pictures all around it. A star, and four hearts to represent me, Jacob, Dad, and a teacher who changed our lives.

www.ingramcontent.com/pod-product-compliance
Lightning Source LLC
Chambersburg PA
CBHW041644070526
44586CB00004B/72